M000073557

GALE
CENGAGE Learning·

Novels for Students, Volume 27

Project Editor: Ira Mark Milne Rights Acquisition and Management: Vernon English, Leitha Etheridge-Sims, Aja Perales, Sue Rudolph Composition: Evi Abou-El-Seoud Manufacturing: Drew Kalasky

Imaging: Lezlie Light

Product Design: Pamela A. E. Galbreath, Jennifer Wahi Content Conversion: Civie Green, Katrina Coach Product Manager: Meggin Condino
© 2008 Gale, Cengage Learning ALL RIGHTS RESERVED. No part of this work covered by the copyright herein may be reproduced, transmitted, stored, or used in any form or by any means graphic, electronic, or mechanical, including but not limited to photocopying, recording, scanning, digitizing, taping, Web distribution, information networks, or information storage and retrieval systems, except as permitted under Section 107 or 108 of the 1976 United States Copyright Act,

without the prior written permission of the publisher.

Since this page cannot legibly accommodate all copyright notices, the acknowledgments constitute an extension of the copyright notice.

For product information and technology assistance, contact us at **Gale Customer Support, 1-800-877-4253.**

For permission to use material from this text or product, submit all requests online at **www.cengage.com/permissions.**

Further permissions questions can be emailed to **permissionrequest@cengage.com** While every effort has been made to ensure the reliability of the information presented in this publication, Gale, a part of Cengage Learning, does not guarantee the accuracy of the data contained herein. Gale accepts no payment for listing; and inclusion in the publication of any organization, agency, institution, publication, service, or individual does not imply endorsement of the editors or publisher. Errors brought to the attention of the publisher and verified to the satisfaction of the publisher will be corrected in future editions.

Gale
27500 Drake Rd.
Farmington Hills, MI, 48331-3535

ISBN-13: 978-0-7876-8684-0
ISBN-10: 0-7876-8684-0
ISSN 1094-3552

This title is also available as an e-book.

ISBN-13: 978-1-4144-3831-3
ISBN-10: 1-4144-3831-1
Contact your Gale, a part of Cengage Learning sales
representative for ordering information.

Printed in the United States of America
1 2 3 4 5 6 7 12 11 10 09 08

The Secret Life of Bees

Sue Monk Kidd 2002

Introduction

The Secret Life of Bees, Sue Monk Kidd's first novel, was published in 2002 and has remained a bestseller since then. Kidd gave up professional nursing to begin her writing career in the form of short inspirational essays for newspapers and magazines. From there, she began writing longer nonfiction books on spiritual transformation and feminist theology. Encouraged by the continuous support of readers and publishers, she turned to writing fiction, combining the spiritual themes she had been exploring with her memories of the southern landscape in which she grew up.

In *The Secret Life of Bees*, the fourteen-year-old narrator, Lily Owens, runs away from home with her African-American nanny at a pivotal moment in southern history, 1964, the height of the Civil Rights movement. Kidd writes in the long tradition of other Southern Gothic storytellers who are known to focus on the elements of the South's decay and moral responsibility. The success of Kidd's first novel led to the publication of a second, *The Mermaid Chair* (2005), which handles the same theme of guilt and redemption. The heroines of both stories seek forgiveness and self-knowledge. In both novels, motifs of the divine feminine make Kidd's contribution to Southern Gothic fiction unique. She illuminates a path out of the harsh legacy of slavery and domination through a feminine viewpoint. *The Secret Life of Bees* is widely used in American classrooms, indicating its timely themes of tolerance and love over power and racism.

Author Biography

Sue Monk Kidd was born Sue Monk on August 12, 1948, and raised in the small town of Sylvester, Georgia, which served as a model for Sylvan, South Carolina, in *The Secret Life of Bees*. As a girl, she listened to her father's stories and began writing stories of her own that were praised by her teachers. Kidd has been a life long journal writer, using the material for her stories and books. Nevertheless, she did not major in English but took a B.S. in nursing in 1970 from Texas Christian University. She worked as a registered nurse in pediatrics and surgery, eventually teaching nursing. She married Sanford Kidd, a theology student, and they had two children, Bob and Ann.

While living in South Carolina where her husband was teaching at a liberal arts college, she enrolled in writing classes in order to write fiction, but when a nonfiction essay of hers was published in *Guideposts*, she began to write personal inspirational pieces. She became a freelancer and editor at *Guideposts*, publishing many articles there and in other magazines and newspapers.

At this time, Kidd began to read widely in literature and spiritual classics, as well as mythology and psychology. Thomas Merton and Carl Jung are two writers who influenced her in these areas. Her first book, *God's Joyful Surprise*, was in the tradition of contemplative spirituality

(1988). *When the Heart Waits*, describing her own spiritual transformation, followed in 1990, and was critically acclaimed. It is this kind of spiritual experience that is woven into her novels.

Her interests broadened to feminist theology and led her to write *The Dance of the Dissident Daughter* in 1996. From there, she took up her old dream of writing fiction and became an accomplished short story writer, studying at Emory and Sewanee and the Bread Loaf Writer's Conference. In 2002, Kidd published her first novel, *The Secret Life of Bees*, and it stayed on the bestseller lists for over two years. It has sold millions of copies and has been translated into twenty-three languages. Her second novel, *The Mermaid Chair*, was published in 2005, and was also a bestseller. In 2006, her early essays were collected and published under the title, *Firstlight: The Early Inspirational Writings of Sue Monk Kidd*. She has served on the board for Poets and Writers, Inc., to encourage emerging writers, and has been Writer-in-Residence at the Sophia Institute in Charleston.

Selected awards include the Book Sense Book of the Year in paperback, 2004, for *The Secret Life of Bees*; the inaugural Literature To Life award presented by The American Place Theatre, 2004; the Quill Award in General Fiction, 2005, for *The Mermaid Chair*; and the Southeastern Library Association Fiction Award in 2005, for *The Secret Life of Bees*.

Chapter 1

Each chapter is headed by an excerpt from manuals on bees that parallel the action in the story. The quote preceding chapter 1 mentions the queen bee as the unifying force of the community. This sets the stage for the story of Lily Owens, age fourteen, and how the loss of her mother at age four fragmented her life.

The story is set in the summer of 1964 in Sylvan, South Carolina, where Lily is living on a peach farm with her abusive father, whom she calls T. Ray, and her African-American nanny, Rosaleen. She recalls the day her mother died in 1954, remembering few details—the suitcase on the floor, the fight her parents had, the gun that she picked up and accidentally set off. The police inquiry calls it a tragic accident.

Lily recounts her misery at school where she has few friends and only the encouragement of her English teacher, who tells her she is smart and should write. She thinks she is unattractive. Her father cannot help her with her adolescent issues, so she turns to Rosaleen, a surrogate mother.

Lily's longing for her mother is like a mystical religion. She has saved relics from her mother's things: a photograph, a pair of gloves, and a postcard of a Black Madonna (the Virgin Mary depicted as an African-American woman) with the place, Tiburon, South Carolina, written on the back. These are buried in a tin box in the orchard. When T. Ray catches her sleeping in the orchard with her box, he punishes her by making her kneel for hours on grits as sharp as ground glass.

That summer, President Johnson signs the Civil Rights Act into law, and Rosaleen walks to town with Lily to register to vote. Rosaleen gets in a fight with some Caucasian men hassling her and is beaten and thrown in jail for stealing fans from the local church.

Chapter 2

The head quote, concerning swarming bees, who leave the old nest and settle nearby to start a new colony, foreshadows Lily's running away from home. Lily and Rosaleen are put into jail, but Lily's father gets her out and leaves Rosaleen there. Lily begs T. Ray to get Rosaleen out too, but he says she is in big trouble, and the man she insulted might kill her. In an argument, T. Ray tells Lily that her mother didn't love her; she was leaving the day she was killed. Lily is in shock. When her father leaves the room, she stares at a jar she left open, hoping the captured bees would fly away. They are gone, and she hears a voice in her mind saying that her own jar is open too. She gathers her things and leaves quickly, catching a ride to town with the church minister. He is on his way to press charges against

Rosaleen for stealing the church fans.

When Lily finds that Rosaleen is in the hospital because the Caucasian men came into the jail and beat her, she goes to the hospital and helps Rosaleen escape. The two hitchhike to Tiburon, South Carolina, chosen because it is the only hint Lily has about her mother. She has a mystical vision of Rosaleen as a kind of Black Madonna when they bathe naked in a creek in the moonlight.

Chapter 3

The bee headnote is the instruction for finding the queen bee: first locate her circle of attendants. Lily wakes up by the creek where she and Rosaleen have spent the night. She calls this day one of her new life. They walk to Tiburon and buy some food at the general store. Lily discovers her mother's picture of the Black Madonna on some jars of honey and asks about them, thinking it is an omen. The storekeeper tells her the honey is made by August Boatwright, a colored woman, and explains how to find her pink house. Walking through Tiburon, they see signs of the times: a sign about Goldwater for President and a bumper sticker supporting the war in Viet Nam. Lily buys a newspaper looking for news of their escape, but it is only full of news of Malcolm X, Saigon, and the Beatles.

Media Adaptations

- *The Secret Life of Bees* was adapted as an unabridged audiobook (read by Jenna Lamia) by HighBridge Audio in 2002.

- *The Secret Life of Bees* was adapted and directed by Wynn Handman. This one-woman stage show was first performed by Denise Wilbanks in 2004.

Chapter 4

Each colony of bees is a family unit, explains the bee headnote. Lily and Rosaleen meet the Boatwright sisters, August, May, and June, African-American women who live on the edge of town on a bee farm. Everything in the large house is rubbed down with beeswax, including the black wooden figure in the corner whom Lily instinctively identifies as a Black Madonna. She feels a magnetic pull to it. Lily makes up lies about why Rosaleen has stitches in her head and what they are doing there. She says her parents are dead, and she is on her way to live with her aunt in Virginia. She asks if there is any work for them so they can earn some money. August says Rosaleen can help May in the house, and Lily can help with the bees.

When May starts to talk about her twin sister April who died, she begins to hum "Oh! Susanna," a distress signal to the other sisters that May is about to go on a crying jag. They send her outdoors to her wailing wall to calm down. The sisters make the refugees at home and give them sleeping cots in the honey house, a garage/factory. Even though Lily has never felt so white, surrounded as she is by African-American women, she feels she belongs in this house. Lily makes Rosaleen promise not to tell about the picture of the Black Madonna. The only strange thing is May's homemade wailing wall with its little bits of paper stuck in the stones, carrying names of the African Americans killed in civil rights demonstrations.

Chapter 5

The headnote speaks of the darkness of beehives. The first week at August's is a relief in Lily's life. August asks no questions but helps the visitors settle in. Lily is trained in beekeeping, as

Rosaleen helps May with the cooking. May is oversensitive to suffering and will not even kill cockroaches. June is a history and English teacher at the African-American high school and plays the cello for dying people. Lily overhears June telling August that they should not have taken the strangers in; everyone is aware Lily is lying. June dislikes Lily because she is Caucasian, and this reverse racism surprises Lily. The soothing fatherly figure of Walter Cronkite giving the news on TV is the opposite of T. Ray in Lily's mind. When, however, Cronkite reports the racial violence that summer, May has a fit. Every night the family kneels before the Black Mary, called Our Lady of Chains.

One evening August tells Lily a story of the nun Beatrix who ran away from the convent. When Beatrix finally returned, humbled, she found the Virgin Mary had stood in for her all those years, so people wouldn't know she was gone. Lily realizes August is trying to tell her something about her own situation, and after that, she begins asking the Virgin Mary for help. August teaches Lily bee etiquette and how to send them love so they won't sting. Lily wants August to love her, so she will keep her. August tells Lily about May's sensitivity stemming from her twin sister's suicide at fifteen when she discovered the suffering of African-American people. At night, Lily longs for her mother. She senses her mother has been here, but Rosaleen warns her, what if Lily finds out something she doesn't want to know?

Chapter 6

The queen bee produces queen substance that attracts the other bees, announces the headnote, introducing the chapter on Our Lady of Chains. Lily meets Neil, the principal of the African-American high school, who wants to marry June. She won't have him, because she was jilted once before at the altar. Lily and June have a private war. On Sunday the sisters host a religious meeting, called the Daughters of Mary. These are local African-American women who show up in colorful costumes that Lily loves to look at. They say Hail Marys, and August tells the story of Our Lady of Chains, as follows.

The statue was once a figurehead of a ship washed up and found by slaves. She looked like a Black Madonna with her fist raised. The slaves believed she had come to give them freedom and worshipped her. She was so powerful, the master hauled her off and chained her up, but she miraculously made her way back to the slaves fifty times without help, until the master gave in and let her stay there. One by one each Daughter of Mary touches the heart of the statue, and Lily longs to touch it too, but June stops playing the cello at that moment, as if to say, you aren't one of us. Lily faints. Walter Cronkite announces the plans for the first moon launch on TV, and August tells Lily this is the end of the moon's mystery. (The moon is where Our Lady lives.)

Chapter 7

The headnote wonders how bees ever became associated with sex. This introduces Lily's meeting with Zach, the teenage African-American boy who helps August with the bees. Zach surprises her by being smart and handsome. He becomes Lily's best friend. Her only problem continues to be June, who is constantly hinting it is time for Lily to be leaving. Lily tells Zach about her love of writing, and he explains he wants to be a lawyer. She has never heard of an African-American lawyer, but Zach tells her you have to imagine what has never been. Rosaleen teases Lily that she is living in a dream world, trying to make this their home. Lily wants to confess everything to August but is afraid she will be sent back to her father.

When Zach and Lily are out on the truck driving around to beehives, Lily begins to be attracted to him. This frightens her because of the racial difference. They visit Mr. Clayton Forrest in Tiburon, the Caucasian lawyer who has befriended Zach. Zach tells Lily about the famous local writer, Willifred Marchant, and Lily is defensive about her own desire to write. He comforts her when she starts to cry, and she puts her head on his shoulder. August tries to help Lily feel comfortable enough to open up, but Lily holds back. Neil and June have a fight and break up. Lily finds herself falling in love with Zach. When he gives her a notebook for her stories, they embrace and remark on how dangerous their affection is. Lily writes stories that feature Rosaleen and August and Zach as heroes.

Chapter 8

The bee headnote says that if a honeybee is isolated from her sisters she will die. Lily settles in to her new life with the Daughters of Mary. August becomes her teacher, showing her the beekeeping business. Lily imbibes a new culture that stems from the Black Madonna, the legacy of the Boatwright grandmother, Big Mama. August tells Lily that Mary is everywhere, inside everything. When Lily asks about her history, August says that both she and June graduated from a Negro college. When August could not get a job, she became a housekeeper in Virginia. Then she inherited the bee farm from her grandmother. She never married because she prefers her freedom.

August shows Lily the beehives and tells her bees have a secret life. If she doesn't want to get stung, she must give love to the bees. Lily has another of her mystical experiences with the bees. She feels they are greeting her as a sister, trying to comfort her. In Tiburon, the racial climate is tense as the movie star, Jack Palance, plans to come to town and integrate the theater by taking an African-American woman with him. Lily remembers the Northerners coming down on a bus in her town to integrate the city pool. Lily wonders why God made different skin pigments. Lily goes with Zach to deliver honey in Tiburon to the lawyer's office. Lily makes a collect call from there to her father, hoping he has missed her. He begins yelling at her, and she hangs up. When Lily gets home, she writes a letter to T. Ray accusing him of being a bad father but tears it up. At night when everyone is asleep, Lily goes to Our Lady of Chains and prays to be fixed.

Chapter 9

The bee headnote mentions that the fabric of bee society depends on communication, implying a lack of it will be the theme of the chapter. Lily says that July 28 was a day for the record books. While Ranger 7 lands on the surface of the moon, and the police look for the bodies of dead civil rights workers, Lily and August water the bees with sugar water because the temperature will be over one hundred degrees that day. Lily gets stung on the wrist by a bee, a sort of initiation into beekeeping. May, Rosaleen, August, and Lily play in the water sprinkler, getting soaked. When June comes out, Lily soaks her with water, and they have a water fight, ending in laughter and forgiveness. Lily and June hug. Lily feels she should tell August about herself but is afraid to spoil the happiness she has found. When she sees May making a trail of graham cracker crumbs and marshmallows to get the roaches out of the house without killing them, Lily is startled, remembering her mother did a similar thing. She wonders if her mother had been here. She asks May if she knew a Deborah Fontenel. May says yes, she stayed in the honey house.

Just as Lily decides she needs to talk to August about her mother, Zach asks her to come to town with him. They see trouble happening between a group of colored boys and some white men. One of the black boys throws a bottle, and the glass cuts a white man. All of the boys are arrested, and no one will say who did it. Zach will have to stay in jail for at least five days before bail can be set. Everyone is angry and worried for Zach, and they decide to keep the news from May. August and Lily visit Zach in jail. Lily promises him that she will write all of these events in a story for him. A few days later, the phone rings and May answers it. It is Zach's mother, who tells May the boy is in jail. May collapses. Then she says she is going to the wailing wall. It is dusk. May takes a flashlight and goes out alone.

Chapter 10

The headnote concerns the shortness of a bee's life. When May is delayed returning from the wall, everyone sets out to find her. They comb the woods while June calls the police. August finds May in the river in two feet of water with a stone on her chest. Lily is nauseated and vomits in the wood. August tells the policeman that May was depressed. He questions Lily, and she lies about who she is and what she is doing there, saying she is an orphan. He does not understand why a Caucasian girl is staying with African-American women and tells her she had better not be there when he returns.

Lily dreams about Zach, but when she wakes, she remembers he is still in jail. The coffin with May in it, fixed up, comes home to the pink house, so May can be mourned properly by the Daughters of Mary. June plays the cello, and Lily feels May's presence in the room. She speaks to her, asking her to look up her mother in heaven with the message to send a sign to Lily that she loves her. Zach arrives, having been let out of jail, and Lily sees something in him has changed.

August, Lily, and Zach go out to drape the hives with black crepe. If the bees stay in the hive, it means the person will live again. August says there are pictures of bees scratched on the walls of catacombs as a symbol of resurrection. When the Daughters of Mary come for the vigil, they make Lily feel like one of them. Lily thinks African-American women are like hidden royalty and doesn't know how they had become so low on the totem pole. May's suicide note is found and she explains to her sisters that she is tired of carrying around the weight of the world. She is going to lay it down. She asks her sisters to live. August tells June it means she must marry Neil.

Chapter 11

The bee fact announced at the beginning of the chapter is that it takes millions of foraging trips to make one pound of honey. This chapter brings together the bits of happiness the characters have earned between them all summer. Now Lily is desperate to have her talk with August about her mother, but August is in her period of mourning and keeps to herself. Neil and June are courting, and Lily and Zach keep company. She wishes she were a Negro girl, but he says they can't change their skins, only the world. He still dreams of being a lawyer. Zach has an angry edge to him now; he speaks of racial tensions and Malcolm X.

When the mourning is over, there is a celebration dinner and evening prayers, and Lily feels the world is back to normal. Lily prepares herself to talk to August about her mother, but she is afraid of being sent to prison for her crime of helping Rosaleen escape. The talk is put off once more, for it is Mary Day the next day, and everyone is baking and decorating. It is a day of thanks when the story of Our Lady of Chains is reenacted. Neil asks June to marry him again, and she says yes. They go off to buy her ring. The Daughters of Mary arrive in the evening and fuss over Lily. They form a circle of feeding and give each other a sort of communion of honey cakes. The statue of Mary is hauled in the wagon, and chained in the honey house for the night as part of the ritual.

Zach and Lily go for a walk by the river, and she asks him not to become mean in his anger at the world. He kisses her. He says he will do everything to become a lawyer, and Lily knows he will, because changes are coming, even to South Carolina. He promises after he makes something of himself, they will be together. He gives her his dog tag.

Chapter 12

The headnote explains the behavior of the queen bee, shy and skittish and perpetually in eternal night, the mother of the hive. This is a chapter about August and Lily's mother, Deborah, the mysterious queen bees of the story. Lily waits in August's room. When August enters, Lily lays out the picture of her mother and asks if they can talk now. August knows who her mother is and says Lily is the spitting image of Deborah. August tells her she worked for the Fontanel family in Virginia and took care of her mother when Deborah was a little girl.

Lily explains why she left home and cries in August's arms. August is like a sponge, absorbing her pain. Lily confesses how she accidentally killed her mother. August tells her that in spite of that, Lily is lovable, and that it seems she was meant to find them. August explains Deborah's background and painful marriage to her father, who was not always so mean. In the beginning, he worshipped her mother and was desolate when she left him. Deborah only married because she was pregnant, and when she felt trapped, she turned to August as a mother, the way Lily turns to Rosaleen. She fled to August's house in Tiburon when Lily was small, because she was falling apart.

Lily says she now hates her mother for leaving her behind. Lily had created a myth about her mother's love, and now she faces the bitter truth that she was an unwanted child. August defends Deborah, saying she had a nervous breakdown, but after three months, Deborah went back home to collect Lily and her things and move to Tiburon. The accident prevented that. August tucks Lily into bed and tells her that nothing is perfect; there is only life.

Chapter 13

A worker bee can fly with a heavier load than herself, explains the headnote. Lily carries the weight of her discovery about her mother in this chapter. The statue of Black Mary is still bound in chains in the honey house, but Lily approaches her for help. She wants someone to understand her devastation and anger at losing her mother. In a fit of anger she flings all the honey jars against the wall and smashes them. Emptied out, she falls asleep by the statue. Rosaleen finds her with blood on her arm, then cleans her up as Lily explains her anger. Lily realizes she could allow this bitterness to take over her life. Rosaleen and Lily clean the honey house before the Daughters of Mary come for the end of the Mary Day ceremony, celebrating Mary's Ascension to heaven.

Neil and Zach unchain the statue and put her on the ground in the sun. They take off her chains, read the Bible, and bathe the statue with honey. This ritual with the other Daughters has a healing effect on Lily. Lily thinks to herself if she could have one miracle from the Bible happen to her it would be to be raised from the dead. August brings Lily a box of her mother's belongings. Among the items is a photo of Deborah with her baby, Lily. Their noses are touching and her mother smiles radiantly. This is the sign of love from her mother that Lily had been looking for.

Chapter 14

The headnote announces that a queenless bee
colony will die, but a new queen can be introduced
to make great change. This comments on Lily's own
healing and acceptance of her divine mother, Mary.
Lily spends time by the river. She muses over all
her hurts and is haunted by her mother. August says
she is grieving. Meanwhile, June plans her wedding
to Neil, and Rosaleen goes to town to register to
vote, to finish what she tried to do in Sylvan. Then
Zach announces he is going to the Caucasian high
school in the fall. Life goes on.

Lily cleans her room and makes an altar with
her mother's things. She has finally made her peace.
The next day she wears her mother's whale pin on
her dress. Her mourning is finished, and she goes to
the beehives with August. One of the hives is
missing a queen. August explains they have to put
in a new queen to save the hive. She also makes the
connection to Lily's situation. If her own mother,
Deborah, is missing, then Our Lady could be the
stand in, she suggests. August says that Our Lady is
not outside but inside of us. August takes Lily's
hand and places it on her own heart.

T. Ray, who traced her from the collect call
from Mr. Forrest's office, finds Lily at the
Boatwrights. She is alone. T. Ray takes out his knife
and stabs the chair in a threatening way, saying he
will take Lily back. Then he sees the whale pin on

her dress and is shocked, for he had given it to Deborah. Lily finally sees how much he must have loved Deborah. T. Ray hits Lily so hard, she falls into Our Lady. He starts calling her Deborah, as though temporarily mad, and she calls him Daddy to snap him out of it. Lily feels she has seen into the dark place in his soul that will never heal. She asserts that she will stay with August. August comes into the room and confirms they love Lily and want her to stay. The Daughters of Mary arrive to stand by Lily, and T. Ray leaves. As T. Ray is pulling out in his truck, Lily runs to ask him if she truly killed her mother. He says that she did, and that it was an accident. She doesn't know if he tells the truth, but she turns back to all the loving women on the porch waiting for her. Clayton Forrest has the charges dropped against Lily and Rosaleen. Lily becomes friends with Clayton's daughter, Becca, and they enroll in the same high school with Zach. Lily continues to write her stories and takes over May's wailing wall, feeding it with prayers. Often she feels Black Mary inside, rising up, filling up the holes life gouges out.

Big Mama

The grandmother of the Boatwright sisters passed on beekeeping and its lore to them when they spent summers on the farm with her as children. She also gave them the wisdom and worship of the Black Madonna, as well as the statue of Our Lady of Chains. Their grandfather then left the farm to August, who was able to stop being a servant and start her business as a beekeeper.

August Boatwright

The eldest Boatwright sister and leader of the Daughters of Mary is the owner of the bee farm and main beekeeper. She makes and sells her Black Madonna honey all over the county. She is tall and dignified, dressed in white like an African bride, when Lily first meets her. She has wire rim glasses and gray hair, is wise and reflective. Lily is surprised to find an African-American person who is so intelligent and well read. August was once a high school teacher like June but never married because she wants her independence. A storyteller and keeper of the myths about the secret life of bees and the Black Madonna, August is the mother figure to whom first Deborah, and then her daughter, Lily, turn in their need. Once the housekeeper for Lily's grandmother in Virginia, she is a respected business woman in Tiburon, South Carolina, with her Black Madonna honey in all the stores and delivered to customers in the truck. She believes in Lily and gives her a chance, making her an apprentice beekeeper. August's elevated status seems to be accepted in the county, for she is not challenged by the local authorities, especially when she harbors Lily. It is a time of fear in the south, but August is unafraid, clearly the queen bee and role model Lily is looking for. Lily feels as if her house is protected by the Black Madonna herself. August's spiritual equilibrium is demonstrated in her leadership of the Daughters of Mary, who rejoice when they are happy, and mourn when they are sad, but never harbor bitterness. August manifests the Madonna's wisdom and protection, balancing out June's excessive intellectual qualities and May's excessive emotional qualities.

June Boatwright

The intellectual and proud sister dislikes Lily at first. She teaches history and English at the colored high school and plays the cello for dying people and at the meetings of the Daughters of Mary. She dates Neil, the African-American principal of the high school who keeps proposing marriage to her, and she keeps refusing because she was once jilted at the altar. Her reverse racism shocks Lily, as she had no idea that African-American people could dislike Caucasians because they were Caucasian. June also dislikes Lily because she can cause trouble for them, and also because her sister August once had to be a servant for Lily's grandmother in Virginia. June is a little embittered, cautious, and does not like to embrace new things. After May's suicide, June marries Neil because May wanted her to live her life fully without fear.

May Boatwright

The emotionally disturbed and oversensitive sister of June and August commits suicide when she hears Zach is in jail. May's twin sister April similarly killed herself at fifteen when she first discovered racial injustice. May will not even kill cockroaches and has kept herself going by creating her wailing wall in the garden as a memorial to sufferers; she writes the names and dates of suffering on slips of paper, and inserts the papers in the cracks. She hums "Oh! Susanna" when she is upset. May is childlike, direct and intuitive and is the first to tell Lily that her mother was in their house. She has braids all over her head and likes to go barefoot. She teaches Lily the honey song, "Place a beehive on my grave" that is sung at her memorial vigil. May is the cook and housekeeper of the family. She is overly compassionate, compared to Mary, with her heart on the outside of her chest.

Rosaleen Daise

Lily's African-American nanny is a former peach orchard worker in Sylvan, whom T. Ray hires to take care of the house after Deborah's death.

Rosaleen is Lily's surrogate mother, and they have a prickly but close relationship. Rosaleen does not go to church, but has made her own religion that is a mixture of nature and ancestor worship. She is rebellious, like Lily herself, and when Rosaleen goes into town to register to vote, gets into trouble with Caucasian men who hassle her. She spits her tobacco juice on their shoes and refuses to wipe it off. She is beaten and thrown in jail, and Lily rescues her and runs away to save her. Rosaleen is special friends with May Boatwright, helping her with cooking and housework. Rosaleen takes May's place after May dies.

Daughters of Mary

The Daughters of Mary include neighbors of the Boatwrights in the Tiburon area: Queenie and her daughter, Violet; Lunelle, who makes outrageous hats; Mabalee; Cressie; and one man, Otis Hill and his wife, Sugar-Girl. They are often joined by Neil and Zach. Colorful, cheerful, eccentric and loving, the Daughters are a circle of devotees that worship God as a woman, as Our Lady of Chains, an old slave legend of the Black Mary. They gather in the Boatwright parlor on Sundays and special holidays. Lily thinks they are special and feels honored to be accepted by them.

Clayton Forrest

The Caucasian lawyer in Tiburon wears red suspenders and a bow tie. He has sandy hair and blue eyes and a friendly smile. He is a good man, who is a friend of the Boatwrights and takes young Zach under his wing, encouraging him to be a lawyer. He helps out in legal matters, such as clearing Zach, Lily, and Rosaleen of possible legal charges against them. His daughter Becca becomes a friend of Lily and Zach's at the Caucasian high school in Tiburon. It is from making a collect call from Mr. Forrest's office that Lily's father is able to trace her.

Avery Gaston

Known as Shoe to the locals, he is the policeman in Sylvan, who appears nice and soft spoken but looks the other way when the Caucasian men come in to beat up Rosaleen in her jail cell. He has the ears of a child, says Lily.

Brother Gerald

The pastor of Ebenezer Baptist Church which Lily and T. Ray attend, is bigoted. Rosaleen and Lily rest there on their way to Sylvan when Rosaleen goes to register to vote. Rosaleen, being African-American, was not supposed to be in the church. Brother Gerald said, we love Negroes in the Lord, but they have their own place. It was so hot that Rosaleen stole the fans from the pew, and Brother Gerald was going to press charges against her, but Lily convinced him that Rosaleen was deaf and didn't know better.

Miss Lacy

The secretary of lawyer Clayton Forrest is about eighty years old and wears fire-red lipstick. It is clear she does not understand what a Caucasian girl like Lily is doing with the Boatwrights. Lily imagines her spreading the rumor all over town.

Willifred Marchant

The famous local author in Tiburon who, Zach says, has won three Pulitzer prizes for her books on deciduous trees of South Carolina. Her books are as esteemed by the Tiburons as the Bible, and every year the schools hold tree planting ceremonies in her name. Lily thinks Zach evokes her as a threat that she will never amount to anything as a writer and cries. Zach comforts Lily, telling her she will be a fine writer.

Neil

No last name is given in the book for the tall, African-American high school principal who is courting June. They work at the same school. He fixes things for the Boatwright sisters, such as their truck, and joins in the ceremonies of the Daughters of Mary. Eventually, June gives in and marries him, for this was May's wish before she died.

Our Lady of Chains

The old blackened ship's masthead in the

parlor of the Boatwright house has the shape of a woman with her fist raised. She is thought to be a Black Madonna. According to legend, she was worshipped as the Virgin Mary by slaves. When taken away by the master and chained up, she miraculously returned to her people each time. She has a sacred heart painted on her chest that is touched during religious services held by the Daughters of Mary. The worship of the statue was passed down by August's grandmother, Big Mama. August, reading about the tradition of Black Mary, used the picture of the Black Madonna of Breznichar, the Bohemian portrait of the Black Virgin, on the honey jars that she sells. She is the Madonna who can release one from bondage, as she gave the slaves hope for freedom and, with her fist raised, represented redress of injustice.

Deborah Fontanel Owens

Lily's mother was the pretty daughter of the widow Sarah Fontanel, in Virginia, where August Boatwright was the housekeeper. Deborah was a somewhat dependent only child, and she clung to August as a mother figure. She moved to South Carolina to be near August when her mother died, and there she unhappily married T. Ray Owens when she became pregnant. She ran away from her husband and child when she was having a nervous breakdown and stayed for a time with the Boatwright sisters. She went back to Sylvan to pack and get Lily, but she was accidentally shot before she could return to the Boatwrights.

Lily Melissa Owens

The first person narrator and main character is a rebellious and spirited girl of fourteen in the summer of 1964, living with her abusive father, T. Ray, on a peach farm. She is implicated in the accidental shooting death of her mother, Deborah, when she was four years old and has been racked with guilt and longing for her mother ever since. Her birthday, July 4th, is the day her transformation begins, when her African-American nanny, Rosaleen, is arrested for insulting Caucasian men. Lily is likeable for her honest voice and passionate spiritual searching. Like May, she is unusually sensitive to the injustice around her, but she has strength and hope that May does not. Though Lily has inherited a bigoted way of life, she is willing to examine it in herself and change. She has a poetic and spiritual way of seeing the beauty around her. Something of an ugly duckling at home in Sylvan, South Carolina, she blossoms at the home of the Boatwright sisters in Tiburon where she runs away. She thinks she is unattractive but finds out she is pretty like her mother. Lily is smart; her English teacher encourages her to write and read. She keeps journals, making stories of her adventures. Imagination is not for escape for her, but is a means of bringing forth something better in life. As she discusses with Zach, one has to imagine what has never been. This ability is what keeps her from becoming bitter or depressed like her father and mother. Rosaleen tells Lily to quit pretending that the Boatwright home is their home, but because she projects so much of her imagination into living there, it does become their new home.

Lily is open to life and to change, and this keeps her moving in the right direction. Her courage is exhibited in the way she gets Rosaleen out of the hospital, and in the way she does not accept a false and cruel life with T. Ray. She refuses to live the hopeless life her mother chose. Though unworldly, she is resourceful and daring when it comes to running away, finding the Boatwrights through pluck and intelligence. Her quest is to find forgiveness and to find mother love, which she does through the Black Madonna. From the beginning, she is given to mystical experiences of places, events, and people. She thinks about God and questions why things are the way they are. Because of this, she receives answers and matures in the course of the novel.

Terrence Ray Owens

Lily calls him T. Ray. Lily's mean father was not always mean. Once loving, he became bitter when the wife he adored, Deborah, ran away and then was accidentally killed, leaving him with their young daughter. He takes his anger out on Lily, refusing to give her love or proper attention. He is bigoted, ignorant, and abuses his power as a white man to get his way. A peach farmer in rural South Carolina with little imagination or sympathy for others, he is moderately successful but an unreliable parent; Lily never knows if he is lying to her. She says he is the opposite of Walter Cronkite, who is her symbol for an honest and caring father figure. T. Ray goes after Lily when she runs away, using violence to try to make her return, but he backs down and leaves her alone when the Daughters of Mary stand by her.

Jack Palance

A movie star who plans to integrate the theater in Tiburon by showing his movie, accompanied by an African-American woman as his date. This upsets the bigots in town and causes the skirmish between the Caucasian men and Zach's friends.

Zachary Lincoln Taylor

Zach is a young African-American man (Lily's age) who works for August, tending the bees on the farm and delivering honey all over the county. He is intelligent and handsome and plans to become a lawyer, even though this was difficult for African Americans at this time. He attends the African-American high school, is an A student, a football player, and likes the jazz musician, Miles Davis, indicating his intellectual tastes. He transfers to a Caucasian high school in the new wave of desegregation. Befriended by Caucasian lawyer Clayton Forrest, who gives him law books and helps him when he is in trouble, Luke is unjustly thrown in jail for something he didn't do, and this injustice is what fuels May's suicide. He is Lily's first boy friend and he encourages her to write. Zach is a model of the young and ambitious African Americans who will emerge from the events of the sixties with new possibilities available to them.

Themes

Racial Intolerance

The action takes place during the summer of 1964 after the signing of the Civil Rights Bill by President Johnson. There are references throughout the book to desegregation and racial violence, beginning with Rosaleen attempting to register to vote. When Rosaleen and Lily are hot, they go into the white Baptist church to cool off, and Brother Gerald, the minister, asks them to leave. Brother Gerald's opinion is that Caucasians can love Negroes, but only in the Lord; they have their own place, not with Caucasians. When Rosaleen announces proudly to the Caucasian men she is going to register to vote, they hassle her, and she spits tobacco juice on their shoes. She is thrown in jail and charged with stealing fans from the church, then she is beat up because the policeman lets the Caucasian men into her cell.

May's wailing wall contains slips of paper with the names and dates of each racial atrocity, as she tries to live with so much injustice and suffering. Her twin sister, April, had killed herself at fifteen when she understood what was in store for her as an African American. The bee farm seems safe with the Black Madonna watching over Lily and her new African-American family, but even a clean cut boy like Zach, who has high aspirations, gets caught up in racial turmoil when his friend throws a bottle that cuts a Caucasian man. Though innocent, Zach stands with his friends in solidarity and goes to jail. The incident begins to make him angry and bitter, illustrating what happens to wound the souls of young African Americans, and how hatred perpetuates itself.

Lily has to confront racial prejudice in herself several times, such as, for instance, when she is surprised that August is intelligent and Zach is handsome. She feels ashamed when she watches the race riots on TV. Lily is completely shocked by her own attraction to an African-American boy. The policeman who tells Lily he doesn't want to see her at the Boatwrights when he comes back refers to a Jim Crow law in South Carolina indicating that no African American can be a guardian for a Caucasian child. In the end, the young people, Lily, Zach, and Becca Forrest, stand for the new trend of desegregation as they attend a Caucasian high school together in the fall as friends.

Topics for Further Study

- Give a report to your class on how conditions have changed in the United States for African Americans since President Johnson signed the Civil Rights Act in 1964, especially in terms of voting, education, and segregation.

- Make a scrapbook with pictures and text about goddesses from different cultural traditions. Write down what you find in common with the religious practices and beliefs of the Daughters of Mary.

- Write an essay that compares and contrasts Lily's spiritual experiences of God to that of saints like Julian of Norwich or Hildegard of Bingen. In what way could Lily and August be thought of as contemplatives (those who find God through inner experience)?

- Compare and contrast the U.S. space program of 1964 with the space program today. How has the space race of the Cold War been replaced by a more cooperative approach? Use visual aids and historic photographs of space missions to illustrate your points in a class presentation.

- Highlight the achievements of African-American leaders in the cause of civil rights from 1955 to 1968. You might give an overview of the development of the Civil Rights movement or focus on some particular figure, like Rosa Parks, Martin Luther King Jr., or Malcolm X. Present your findings in a report.

- Read another story or novel in the Southern Gothic genre by a female writer (Harper Lee, Flannery O'Connor, Carson McCullers, etc.). In an essay, compare and contrast the settings, characters, and plot to *The Secret Life of Bees*.

Need for Parental Love

Lily is starved for parental love and guidance. She confesses the tragedy of her life, the accidental shooting of her mother when she was four, and her constant prayer, "Mother, forgive." Lily is desperate for a mother's love and creates her own myth and worship of her mother, hoarding a few objects, such as a picture of her mother, and a postcard of the Black Madonna from Tiburon. Her impetus for running away is as much to find a sign that her mother loved her, as to save Rosaleen, who is a maternal surrogate.

Similarly, Lily is also missing a father, for though she lives with him, he ignores and abuses her. T. Ray is a bully, punishing Lily for the slightest offense, making her kneel for hours on grits as sharp as ground glass in order to humble and humiliate her. She sees the same sneer on her father's face as on the face of the racists who heckle Zach: "the sort of look conjured from power without benefit of love." He is a bigot, ignorant of the rights of others. In this way, the theme of parental love is widened to include a larger social scope as well. By contrast, Lily singles out Walter Cronkite on the evening news as a soft spoken and reliable father figure for the whole nation. Surely, Cronkite cares and tells the truth, unlike her father who lies to her. The Caucasian lawyer, Clayton Forrest, is a good father towards his own daughter, and Zach and Lily as well.

There is a hole in Lily's heart from not having parental love, especially mother love, but August teaches her that if one's earthly mother is not dependable, there is always a heavenly mother. Lily turns to the Black Madonna, through the circle of the Daughters of Mary, to be healed.

Guilt and Redemption

Lily has anger towards her parents, but she has guilt as well, especially towards her mother, as she feels responsible for her mother's death. There is no one in Lily's young world to help her bear or understand this kind of guilt. She uses her imagination to help her survive, imagining meeting her mother in heaven and writing stories, inventing her own myths about her mother and inventing secret ceremonies in the orchard with the buried mementos. Lily's guilt makes her both vulnerable and self-deprecating. She does not believe she is good or deserves much kindness because of her crime. At the same time, she is rebellious. She yearns for acceptance and forgiveness.

August becomes not only a mother, but a sort of spiritual teacher for Lily. She tells Lily about the secret life of bees, which includes the secrets of human life as well. The beekeeping lore and the lore of the Black Madonna give Lily new archetypes, a new religion of strength, love, and forgiveness. For instance, August tells Lily that she must give the bees love so she won't be stung: "Every little thing wants to be loved." At first, the bees do not sting Lily when she loves them. She also has to learn that sometimes even when one gives love, bees sting anyway. Big Mama said that is why women make good beekeepers; they understand the stings from taking care of families.

Lily confesses killing her mother to August, who tells her it was a terrible accident and takes her in her arms and says she loves her. This confession and absolution start Lily's healing. In the beginning, it is Lily who must be forgiven for killing her mother. After she learns she was unwanted, she is angry, and it is she who must forgive her mother. August tells her, "There is nothing perfect … There is only life."

Lily goes through a period of mourning once she learns the truth about her mother's temporary desertion. She is empty and drained out, ready to be filled again. During the Mary Day celebration the Daughters chant "We will rise." Lily desires to be miraculously brought back from the dead, as in the Bible. August finds a box of Deborah's belongings in which there is a picture of Deborah and Lily together. It is obvious from her mother's expression that Deborah loves her child. This is the sign Lily has looked for. People would rather die than forgive, because they come to love their wounds, Lily reflects. But not wanting to become bitter like her father, she chooses forgiveness. August tells her she must not only love, but persist in love. Lily, using her many religious epiphanies with the bees and Our Lady, is able to forgive herself and her mother, and even her father. August teaches her that she is divine, that God and forgiveness are inside.

God as Mother

Lily was raised a Baptist and had hardly ever heard of the Mother of God, who only appears at Christmas in the Protestant doctrine. By the end of the summer, she has experienced the truth August tells her: the divine Mother, the Black Madonna, goes into the holes life has gouged out of us. August teaches her to experience God as Mother in the religion of the Daughters of Mary. Lily has her own homemade mother religion before she even meets August, that includes the mysterious postcard of the Black Madonna her mother got in Tiburon. She makes a myth of how her mother loved her and imagines speaking to her in heaven. When they run away, she has a vision of Rosaleen naked in the stream in moonlight, and it is a prefiguration of the Black Madonna she is about to discover in Tiburon.

On Sundays, the Boatwrights hold services so the congregation, the Daughters of Mary, can touch the sacred heart of Mary on the statue of Our Lady of Chains to receive grace. Mary Day, celebrating Mary's Ascension to heaven, is the main ceremony that allows Lily to rise from her spiritual death to a rebirth. It begins with the circle of feeding, a new sort of communion, where each one feeds the other honey cakes, symbolizing sharing and nurturing, both of which are maternal traits.

Southern Gothic

The Gothic novel, or supernatural mystery story, that took its name from the spooky Gothic mansions of its settings, originated in eighteenth and nineteenth century Europe and was adapted to fiction that takes place in the Southern United States. The style may include old mansions, threats of violence, grotesque characters, death or a murder mystery, the theme of decay, an appeal to the supernatural, a haunting past with family secrets, omens and prophesies, and a spiritual or moral dimension. William Faulkner, Flannery O'Connor, Carson McCullers, Harper Lee, and Truman Capote are among writers of this genre. *The Secret Life of Bees* has some of these elements, such as the omens Lily sees around her: prophesies, such as bees swarming before a death; T. Ray's cruel character; May's suicide; the threat of racial violence; the mystery of Deborah's death; and the miraculous powers of Our Lady of Chains. The book is reminiscent of Scout's adventures in *To Kill a Mockingbird*, by Harper Lee. Scout confronts the evil in human nature the way Lily does, and both young heroines triumph, finding faith in life's continuance and renewal, despite cruelty and ignorance around them. Because of their own generosity and goodness, they see it in others, and receive it in turn. Like Scout's story, Lily's takes place in small southern towns full of bigoted characters. Atticus Finch, the liberal white lawyer in Harper Lee's story, is similar to Clayton Forrest in Kidd's novel.

Bildungsroman

The Secret Life of Bees is fashioned primarily as a bildungsroman, a coming of age novel, showing the emergence of a young person and their shift in views to see the world in a more adult perspective. In the bildungsroman, the main character's growth is chronicled, step by step, from innocence to experience. Usually, the hero or heroine must discover that life is not black and white, but mixed, and must learn to accept responsibility for his or her own life, rather than living a false, conventional life. This novel form became popular in the nineteenth century with such examples as *David Copperfield* by Charles Dickens and *Jane Eyre* by Charlotte Brontë. *Huckleberry Finn* by Mark Twain, for instance, has a similar innocent first person narrator whose perspective is more direct and truthful than an adult's, thus laying bare hypocrisy and injustice. Like Huck Finn, Lily is the young Caucasian person who runs away with an older African-American servant. Huck and Jim in Twain's novel, and Lily and Rosaleen in Kidd's novel, become friends in a treacherous and bigoted southern landscape. Both Huck and Lily have to overcome what they have been taught about the place of African Americans, using their own humane intuition and moral judgment. Their growth points to the larger moral growth needed in society.

Spiritual Memoir

One of Kidd's mentors was Henry David Thoreau, who wrote nonfictional spiritual memoir. *Walden* is assigned to Lily by Mrs. Henry, her English teacher. Like Thoreau, Lily does not just tell autobiographical incidents from her life but teases out the moral and spiritual implication of everything that happens to her. This is primarily achieved through paralleling the life of bees to human life, highlighted in the headnotes to each chapter. Thoreau had a similar habit of seeing spiritual laws in natural phenomena, such as a river rising in spring as a proof of the eternal resurrection of the spirit. Similarly, the secret life of bees contains the wisdom of life; for instance, the hive cannot survive without its mother or queen bee, symbolizing the search for mother. Lily ultimately must find the queen, or mother, within. Finding the spiritual truth within oneself is the message of many spiritual memoirs, a form popular today for its inspirational power.

Racial Tension

May's homemade wailing wall in the backyard of the Boatwright house in *The Secret Life of Bees* makes sense in terms of the historic context of the summer of 1964. This was the time when the efforts towards desegregation in the south were heating up, and there was much violence as protesters were thrown in jail or killed on the streets. The civil rights of African Americans were dearly bought, and May's heartbreaking notes stuck in her wall, memorialize the sacrifice. Racial tension in the United States is nothing new, but it is important to remember that, although African Americans had the legal right to vote, in the 1950s and early 1960s, when the Civil Rights movement began to take shape, African Americans were barred from registering to vote in the south and from running for office. At the same time, segregation made it impossible for African Americans to mingle with Caucasians in any public place. One must imagine separate restaurants, movie theaters, schools, churches, hotels, and parks. African-American citizens had little legal recourse for injustice. The federal court ruled segregation in schools unconstitutional in 1954, but it was still in practice. If African Americans were arrested and thrown in jail, it was common for them to be beaten and held without charges. Lily is like many Caucasians at this time, barely aware of the problem, for she lives on the privileged side of the fence. African Americans, like Rosaleen, and even August, were employed and taken for granted as nannies, housekeepers, cooks, and workers, much as in slave days. Zach's dream of becoming a lawyer is a revelation for Lily.

Demonstrations and the Civil Rights Act

In 1955, Rosa Parks in Montgomery, Alabama, broke the rule that African Americans had to sit in the back of the bus and she was arrested as a result. It was the spark that set off demonstrations and sit-ins by African Americans everywhere to win their civil rights. In 1962, when African-American James Meredith tried to attend the University of Mississippi by federal court order, two people were killed and twenty-nine marshalls shot trying to protect him. Zach's act of attending a Caucasian high school in Tiburon thus shows great courage. In 1963, the Children's Crusade, with thousands of African-American high school student protesters, was attacked by fire hoses and police dogs in Birmingham. The violence roused public outrage. The 1963 march on Washington, DC, where Dr. Martin Luther King, Jr., delivered his famous "I Have a Dream" speech was attended by 200,000 people and made a huge impact on public awareness, yet it was not until July 2, 1964, that President Johnson was able to get the Civil Rights

Act passed. This bill barred discrimination in public places, and mentioned voting rights, but voter's rights were addressed more fully in the Voting Rights Act of 1965, which suspended the poll taxes, literacy tests, and other measures that had kept African Americans from voting. Within months, a quarter of a million African Americans, like Rosaleen, registered to vote, and within four years, voter registration in the south doubled, as African Americans entered the political scene as a new force.

Compare & Contrast

- **1964:** Ranger 7 lands on the moon to send back pictures of the surface in the aggressive space race between the United States and Soviet Union during the Cold War.
  Today: U.S. astronauts take their spacewalk from the international space station, containing American and Soviet astronauts working together to create a permanent orbiting science institute in space.

- **1964:** Jim Crow laws in the south, proclaiming separate but equal status, prevent African-American students from attending white schools. During the Civil Rights Movement many Americans, African-American and Caucasian, are killed in demonstrations when African-American students try to integrate into Caucasian high schools and colleges.

Today: African-American students are free to attend the schools of their choice, though inequities still exist, as for example, the low number of African-American faculty members in higher education.

- **1964:** Four years before his assassination, despite his arrests and time in jail, at the age of thirty-five, Martin Luther King Jr. is the youngest man to receive the Nobel Peace Prize.

  Today: Frequently compared to Lincoln in terms of his martyrdom, Martin Luther King Jr. is celebrated as one of the great patriots of his country. His birthday is a national holiday and is honored with as much importance as Lincoln's and Washington's birthdays.

- **1964:** Beekeeping is a local and ancient art. The usual beekeeping problems are stings, swarming hives, and regional weather patterns affecting honey production.

  Today: Beekeeping is commercialized, and the number of independent beekeepers has dropped. The first national bee crisis is reported and labeled as "Colony Collapse Disorder." Worker bees suddenly abandon the hive, possibly because of climate change, pesticides, or the stress of over production, thus threatening the pollination necessary for agriculture.

Violence

The Secret Life of Bees opens with the announcement of the Civil Rights Act of 1964, and that summer was a crucial one for the cause. Lily says, "Since Mr. Johnson signed that law, it was like somebody had ripped the side seams out of American life." It was Mississippi Freedom Summer where Caucasian college students from the north came in buses to help register African Americans to vote and to teach in Freedom Schools. The murder of four of those students is mentioned in the novel. Dr. Martin Luther King, Jr., won the Nobel Peace Prize in 1964 for his nonviolent methods of creating change, but his future martyrdom in 1968 is referred to in Rosaleen's dream of the red spit in his mouth painting her toenails. It was a decade of assassinations: President John F. Kennedy in 1963, Malcolm X in 1965, Dr. King and Robert Kennedy in 1968. Meanwhile, there were race riots in northern cities like New York and Philadelphia and later in Watts, Los

Angeles. African-American militancy was born in the Black Power groups and Malcolm X's ideas of African-American self-sufficiency appealed to many younger African Americans, who, like Zach, were impatient with slow change.

The Music of the 1960s

The reference to the Beatles, English pop stars, highlights mainstream music of the time, yet Zach listens to Miles Davis, one of the most influential African-American jazz musicians of the twentieth century, who pioneered cool jazz and jazz fusion. Zach signals his sophistication in admiring the intellectual Davis, who, though famous and respected throughout the world, still suffered the indignity of being beaten by a policeman in 1959 for appearing with a Caucasian woman in public— an event that made him bitter, as Zach becomes bitter after being arrested.

The Space Race

The space race, illustrated by the Ranger 7 flight in chapter 6, was a real political issue in the 1960s, as the United States and the Soviet Union competed to reach the moon first. Not only would such an achievement create prestige but it would display technical mastery in the Cold War. The Soviets seemed to be ahead in the early 1960s with their manned flights. The American Ranger 7 missile, launched the summer of 1964, was one of a series designed to explore the moon; it sent back

4,300 pictures showing the moon surface to be dominated by craters. These launches prepared for the actual moon landing in 1969. August Boatwright echoes a popular sentiment that the moon launches destroy the mystery of the moon, which she associates with Mary.

The Vietnam War

During the 1960s, the Vietnam conflict was in full force, another result, like the space race, of Cold War tension. The civil war in Vietnam between the Northern communist government in Hanoi and the Southern democracy of Saigon was taken as a proving ground between the Americans and Soviets. In 1964, the American involvement was escalating, and it was not until 1975 that Americans finally withdrew from their only military defeat. The anti-war movement at home is not mentioned in the novel, but Americans were furious at so much money and so many lives being wasted abroad when there was so much need at home. With these dramatic events, Kidd connects the events in Lily's life to the life of the country as a whole, as a moment of coming of age, in which the country must reflect on its priorities and aggressive methods, as well as its loss of mother consciousness.

Critical Overview

From its first publication in 2002, the book was a bestseller and was critically acclaimed in reviews throughout the country. Adam Mazmanian's article in the *New York Times Book Review* is typical. "Lily is a wonderfully petulant and self-absorbed adolescent, and Kidd deftly portrays her sense of injustice as it expands to accommodate broader social evils," he states. Most readers agree with Mazmanian's assessment that the characters are "fully imagined." An article in the *Virginia Quarterly Review* describes the book as a "gem of a first novel" and mentions that the book is "rich in symbolism and feminine adaptations of devout religious practices … a captivating story of self-discovery …" A critique in the *Southern Literary Review* approves the plot and theme: "This well-written novel is a poetic coming-of-age story about mothers—the need for mothers, the need to know our mothers and the need to be mothers." Enthusiasm for the novel has spilled over to college and high school curriculums, many of which now list the novel as required reading for classes. A book review by Penny Stevens in *School Library Journal* gives a feel for why the novel is embraced by educators: "There is a wonderful sense of the strength of female friendship and love throughout the story."

What Do I Read Next?

- Clarissa Pinkola Estés, included in Kidd's own reading lists, is the author of a classic study of popular myths from European and native cultures that explain how woman's nature is either compromised or set free. *Women Who Run with the Wolves: Myths and Stories of the Wild Woman Archetype* was published in 1992.

- Sue Monk Kidd's *Firstlight: The Early Inspirational Writings of Sue Monk Kidd* contains short personal anecdotes of the spiritual significance of everyday occurrences, all held together by a new essay, "The Crucible of Story" that advocates storytelling as a method of spiritual growth. It was published in 2006.

- Kidd's second novel *The Mermaid Chair* contains similar themes to her first: a woman who thinks she caused a parent's death; forbidden love; and a mystery. The difference here is that the main character is a woman in her forties undergoing a midlife crisis. The book was published in 2005.

- *To Kill a Mockingbird* (1960), by Harper Lee, is an important predecessor to *The Secret Life of Bees*. Six-year-old tomboy Scout Finch is, like Lily, another innocent who faces the absurdities of Southern prejudice.

Sources

Bloxham, Laura J., Review of *The Secret Life of Bees*, in *Dialog: A Journal of Theology*, Vol. 44, No. 2, Summer 2005, pp. 197-98.

Brown, Rosellen, "Honey Child," in the *Women's Review of Books*, Vol. 19, No. 7, April 2002, p. 11.

Jones, Ann Goodwyn, "Women Writers and the Myths of Southern Womanhood," in *The History of Southern Women's Literature*, edited by Carolyn Perry and Mary Louise Weaks, Louisiana State University Press, 2002, p. 280.

Kidd, Sue Monk, "A Conversation with Sue Monk Kidd," in *The Secret Life of Bees*, Penguin, 2003, Appendix, pp. 4-14.

————, *The Dance of the Dissident Daughter*, HarperCollins, 1996, pp. 16, 75-83.

————, *Firstlight: The Early Inspirational Writings of Sue Monk Kidd*, GuidepostsBooks, 2006, pp. 16, 20-21, 70.

————, *The Secret Life of Bees*, Penguin, 2003.

————, *When the Heart Waits: Spiritual Direction for Life's Sacred Questions*, HarperCollins, 1992, pp. 87, 102, 124, 158-63, 189.

Maryles, Daisy, "Kidd Kudos," in *Publishers Weekly*, April 18, 2005, http://www.publishersweekly.com.article/CA525302 (accessed July 27, 2007).

Mazmanian, Adam, Review of *The Secret Life of Bees*, in the *New York Times Book Review*, March 31, 2002, Vol. 151, No. 52074, p. 17.

Review of *The Secret Life of Bees*, in the *Southern Literary Review*, http://www.southernlitreview.com/reviews/the_secre (accessed July 27, 2007).

Review of *The Secret Life of Bees*, in the *Virginia Quarterly Review*, Vol. 78, No. 3, Summer 2002, p. 91.

Stevens, Penny, Review of *The Secret Life of Bees*, in the *School Library Journal*, Vol. 48, No. 5, May 2002, p. 179.

Further Reading

Christ, Carol P., *Diving Deep and Surfacing: Women Writers on Spiritual Quest*, Beacon Press, 1980.

> Christ is one of Kidd's influences, and she insists that women tell their spiritual stories. She analyzes stages of awakening in the works of the authors Kate Chopin, Margaret Atwood, Doris Lessing, Adrienne Rich, and Ntozake Shange.

Thoreau, Henry David, *Walden, or Life in the Woods*, Princeton University Press, 1989.

> Thoreau's classic tale of finding his higher self at Walden pond was influential on Kidd and on her character, Lily. In it, Thoreau shares the spiritual lessons he has learned from nature.

Walker, Alice, *The Color Purple*, Washington Square Press, 1982.

> This is Walker's Pulitzer Prize winning novel about the life of African Americans in rural Georgia. Sometimes criticized for its explicit sex and violence, it is uplifting in its depiction of the spiritual triumph of a poor African-American woman,

Celie.

X, Malcolm, and Alex Haley, *The Autobiography of Malcolm X*, Grove Press, 1965.

> Malcolm X, a Civil Rights leader, details his memories of the period in which Kidd's novel is set. The autobiography details Malcolm X's rise from drug dealer to African-American spiritual and political leader.